MISM

The ISIM Papers represent individual lectures delivered at the ISIM. The aim of this series is both to allow the papers, initially presented before limited audiences, to be shared by the entire academic community and to contribute to the further development of the study of Islam in the modern world.

Published by:
International Institute for the Study of Islam in the Modern World (ISIM)

Series Editor:
Dick Douwes

ISIM PAPERS:

1. James Piscatori
   Islam, Islamists, and the Electoral Principle in the Middle East

2. Talal Asad
   Thinking about Secularism and Law in Egypt

3. John Bowen
   Shari'a, State, and Social Norms in France and Indonesia

4. Barbara D. Metcalf
   'Traditionalist' Islamic Activism: Deoband, Tablighis, and Talibs

5. Abdulaziz Sachedina
   The Role of Islam in the Public Square: Guidance or Governance?

6. Lila Abu-Lughod
   Local Contexts of Islamism in Popular Media

LOCAL CONTEXTS OF ISLAMISM IN POPULAR MEDIA

Lila Abu-Lughod

ISIM PAPER 6

AMSTERDAM UNIVERSITY PRESS
ISIM / LEIDEN

Cover design and lay-out: De Kreeft, Amsterdam

ISBN 90 5356 824 7
ISSN 1568-8313
NUR 717

Local Contexts of Islamism in Popular Media[1]

This ISIM Annual Lecture was delivered on 17 December 2004 at the Spiegelzaal, Utrecht University.

A good deal of literature, before and since the publication of Edward Said's *Orientalism* and then *Covering Islam*, has taught us the myriad ways in which Islam has been represented negatively in the West. Those of us who have observed media representations in the US since the attacks on 11 September 2001 can hardly avoid the conclusion that an even more simplistic oppositional discourse has become hegemonic, one that by and large reduces Islam to Islamists, but will not even dignify the complex and multiple worldviews and politics to which such a label might gesture. Instead, this discourse resorts to the nonspecific and ahistorical – and even history-denying – label of "terrorist" to describe an astonishingly wide range of Muslims and those who study them. The label terrorist is used to describe individuals and groups using violence to challenge repressive regimes, occupation forces, and imperial powers. The label "terrorist" is applied to both secular and explicitly Islamic Middle Eastern regimes not under the sway of the US. This label is even stretched to include individual scholars who themselves argue only that political Islam deserves serious analysis. Some of these are denied visas so that they cannot accept professorships in the US; others are denounced on websites like the notorious right-wing Campus Watch that monitors scholars who work on Islam and the Middle East, ever vigilant against scholarly and nuanced studies of Islam or representations of Israel that are not rightwing and zealously Zionist.

What is profoundly disturbing about this labeling is that it has revived, in a simple form, a profoundly civilizational discourse. It re-inscribes a barely disguised opposition between a now vulnerable West of freedom and civility (where many people, even colleagues of mine in the university, heed the multicolored

1. This text is derived largely from Chapter 7 of Lila Abu-Lughod's recent book, *Dramas of Nationhood: The Politics of Television in Egypt* (University of Chicago Press, 2005). Full acknowledgments and references may be found in the book.

alert system devised by the US government to generate fear and justify violence abroad and curtailments of civil rights at home) and an irrational and deeply disturbing Muslim East that breeds those who attack without reason. No historical narratives are allowed, no complex analysis of histories of geopolitical interaction can be countenanced.

But what interests me – an anthropologist who has worked in Egypt for the last 25 years, and who has spent more than a decade researching Egyptian television in particular – is the way Islamists have been depicted in the Middle East. After all, it is true that in the 1980s and early 1990s, long before the spectacular and specular violence of the exploding World Trade Center in New York City, many countries in the Arab Middle East had within their midst Islamist political groups that were opposed to the regimes in power. In Egypt during the 1980s and 90s, for example, there was a sharp sense in elite circles and a widespread discourse disseminated through popular media that the nation was in danger of being torn apart from within. The state was portrayed as facing a political-cultural crisis, one that it dealt with mostly by force – through arrests, executions, and the arbitrary powers of a continually renewed state of emergency. The problem was represented publicly as religious extremism. The villains were the members of Islamic groups.

In the early 1990s, I embarked on an ethnographic project to understand television's place in the Egyptian national imagination and in the everyday lives of people who are somewhat marginal to the nation – people who are not middle class, or not urban. I focused on the most popular genre of television programming, the genre for which Egypt is justly famous across the Arab world, the dramatic serial. Unlike soap operas, Egyptian serials are finite, consisting of 15 or 30 episodes, shown on consecutive evenings. And, because until well into the 1990s, there were only a few television channels with first-run serials aired on only two of them, they were watched by a majority of the population and were often the subject of discussion in homes, as well as in the public sphere, in newspapers, magazines, and elsewhere. I was intrigued to discover that television serials were often the vehicles for national debate. One of the big debates that television became part of in the mid-1990s was about what was called "extremism" or even "terrorism." So it ended up as one of several aspects of television that I studied.

It turned out that television drama in Egypt in the 1990s reflected, if unevenly and with certain lags, concerns about the place of religion in society and nation. In keeping with its self-consciously pedagogical mission, television drama condemned, preached, and offered up alternative models for the future. I am going to talk about two of the three strategies major television dramas of the 1990s followed for treating religious extremism. Two of these strategies – discrediting terrorists and modeling forms of Coptic-Muslim unity – were, I think, pursued deliberately, with government sanction. The third, which involved recuperating "traditional" rural cultural values, appears to have been somewhat more serendipitous but is important because it offered up "authentic" positive alternatives to Islamic identity from and for Upper Egypt, the very region most associated in the minds of the northern urban elite with Islamic militancy.

The obvious question is whether these strategies were effective in their missions of smoothing over the divisions that, in the name of religion, threatened the Egyptian national body. Does this media management of religion help create national community? A more complex and important question is how mass media may have participated in the configuration and reconfiguration of "religion" in Egypt. Can religion any longer be understood without reference to the nation-state? The third question, however, is one that my concerns about Western media representations of Islamists raise. How do media representations of Islamic groups and "terrorists" operate in a Muslim majority context where the civilizational discourse of West and East cannot be mobilized, where Islamists or terrorists can only partially be represented as an outside enemy and Islam can never be the alien other. In this paper, I am going to try to address all three questions.

Good and bad Islam

Writers of Egyptian television drama often take their ideas from the life they find around them. It was therefore remarkable to me that during the period of my research from 1989 to 1993, there was no treatment in television drama of the phenomenon that was noticeable to everyone beginning in the late 1970s and troubling to some: the rising visibility on the streets of Cairo and provincial cities and towns of a self-conscious Islamic identity and move toward piety, especially among educated youth, not to mention some more sensational acts of violence committed by militant Islamic groups. The first phase of this violence is epitomized for many in Egypt and abroad by the assassination of Egypt's second president, Anwar Al-Sadat, in 1981. The second phase began in the early 1990s in the form of a campaign to weaken the regime by hitting at Egypt's tourist industry. It involved attacks on tourist buses, especially in Upper Egypt, and was followed by skirmishes – some call it a feud, as I will discuss below – with the government security forces in major cities of Upper Egypt such as Asyut and Sohaj. The third phase, dramatized by the World Trade Center attack of 2001, seems to have taken the form of exported violence, some of it directed at the US. This phase owes much to the suppression of these groups at home and their exclusion from political power or participation.[2]

In the late 1980s and early 1990s, when I began my research, the most talked about serials were silent on the issue of Islamism.[3] Instead, they were concerned with issues of patriotism, citizenship and the law, culture, and Egyptian history. All that viewers could see were people for whom religion was taken for granted as part of their identity and that sometimes offered solace in times of personal trouble. Piety was seen only among the elderly.

That the avoidance of any representation of Islamists, the piety movement, and religious youth on television was due in part to the censorship to which television dramas are subjected, both from the censor's office of the Egyptian Radio and Television Union and "higher up," became clear when official policy suddenly shifted.[4] In 1993, newspapers trumpeted the new policy announced by the Minister of Information of "confronting terrorism with media." As with most political moves, the policy was cleverly satirized by Egypt's best cartoonists in popular periodicals. One cartoon shows two men chatting in a café. One says to the other, "Those terrorists have really overdone it. But they're not up to Safwat al-Sharif (the minister of information in charge of state television). He could hit 'em with two serials that'd knock 'em flat!"

It suddenly became acceptable for a writer like the fantastic Usama Anwar 'Ukasha, who had earlier battled with censors over the inclusion of a scene in a mosque (intended to show the early development of the Islamist movement) to feature a misguided young man who had joined an extremist Islamic group as a key character. He also showed how two characters who had collaborated with the British became suddenly "pious" but only to swindle people through their Islamic investment company.[5] This appeared in a major Ramadan hit serial, *Hilmiyya Nights* (and for those of you who do not know this, Ramadan is the biggest TV season, when all the best serials are aired and people watch late into the night). More telling, in 1994, a serial whose screenplay had been allegedly held up for three years was produced with great fanfare, and some controversy.[6] Called *The*

2. Timothy Mitchell, "McJihad: Islam in the US Global Order," *Social Text* 73 (2002): 1-18.
3. For more on this, see Abu-Lughod, "Finding a Place for Islam," *Public Culture* 5 (1993): 493-513.
4. Another part of the explanation, everyone is quick to add, is the constraints felt by private producers of television serials who must be able to sell dramas to Saudi Arabia and the wealthy Gulf states, where moral and political censorship is more restrictive.
5. See Abu-Lughod, "Finding a Place for Islam."
6. 'Imad 'Abd al-Rahman, "Waqa'i' muhawalat ightiyal musalsal al-'a'ila" (The facts about the attempt to assassinate the serial *The Family*), *Akhbar al-Adab*, March 20, 1994, 1, 5-7.

Family (*al-'a'ila*), the serial was written by Wahid Hamid, and showed Islamist groups in a very bad light, using popular and well-known actors.

A close look at the discussion of this serial in the Egyptian press reveals not just the strategies pursued in this new media campaign but something the public reception makes very clear: that multiple positions have been taken regarding the campaign itself. Most of the articles, especially in the official press, were positive. Some reported on reactions of people on the streets, especially in the poorer neighborhoods that had a strong Islamist presence. Those quoted praised the serial with comments like the following: "The serial *The Family* shook all the families of Egypt and helped parents become aware of the nascent danger by warning them and enabling them to protect their children from these groups." Such responses corresponded to the critics' assessment of the serial as showing how educated youth from disadvantaged backgrounds were drawn into terrorism, and how corruption is rife in these groups.[7] Even the actors who starred in the serial stressed its pedagogical value. The actor playing the lead character explained: "The religious path can never be violent... I think we need to admit there is a 'lack of awareness' among people that has left an empty field to be filled by words said in the name of religion. This is what facilitates irrational terrorism. It is also precisely why we need strong attempts at raising awareness. I think – I am sure – that this serial provides one such means of consciousness raising."

Public opposition, not surprisingly, came from well-established moderate Islamist thinkers like the one who wrote a long piece criticizing the serial for not distinguishing between extremism and religiosity. As he explained in the Muslim Brotherhood opposition newspaper *Al-Sha'b* in 1994, there is a basic struggle in Egypt between secularists who, "wish to cantonize religion in places of worship and refuse to allow it to enter into all aspects of life" and Islamists who "wish to follow the understanding and principles of Islam in all aspects of their life." The latter, he added, differ little from the average Muslim. His analysis was that the ongoing struggle between the ruling factions of the government and a small extremist faction of Islamists had enabled secularists (like the writer of this serial) to get away with vilifying Islam and ridiculing all forms of piety.[8] Another Islamist writer in the same newspaper shared this position. He accused the serial of mocking millions of viewers by ridiculing their religion. He was

7. Salah Mursi, "Al-sinima wa qadiyat al-watan" (Cinema and the case of the nation), *Al-Musawwar*, March 18, 1994, 46-47.
8. Muhammad Ibrahim Mabruk, "Musalsal al-'a'ila... wa ish'al nar al-fitna bayn al-muslimin" (The serial *The Family*... and inflaming sedition among Muslims), *Al-Sha'b*, March 22, 1994, 9.

particularly incensed that the serial misrepresented Islam as the religion of the poor and powerless. The effusive response in the press was, for him, part of "a brain-washing campaign" initiated by the Minister of Interior to attack the Islamist movement.

In their jockeying in the press, both the moderate Islamist thinkers and government and television officials tried to align themselves with the religious authorities of al-Azhar, the major religious establishment of Egypt (and the wider Muslim world). A mosque and university that has been the seat of Islamic learning since the eleventh century, al-Azhar has also become one of the important voices of official Islam, with its tangled relationship to the state in the twentieth century. The desire to align themselves with al-Azhar was due to its popular image as representing the orthodox authority of religion, even though in recent decades it has been criticized by Islamists for being under the state's thumb and has been regarded with some anxiety by the state for harboring scholars with strong Islamist sympathies.[9] The Islamists stressed the number of letters and phone calls al-Azhar had received, urging them to take action to take the serial off the air. They demanded to know why the script had not first been sent to al-Azhar for approval. Controversy over a scene in which the enlightened modernist challenges the extremist on the doctrinal basis of certain beliefs led to calls to halt the broadcast of the serial and even responses in the press by the Mufti, the leading government religious authority, clarifying doctrine and offering a set of phone numbers for the public to use if they had questions about religious matters.

On the other hand, the government and television officials also tried to align themselves with al-Azhar, constructing themselves as the preservers of proper, as opposed to excessive or incorrect, Islam. The government strategy to align itself with proper Islam and al-Azhar became clearer in the following months. Just as *The Family* ended, television channels broadcast the videotaped confessions of a repentant Islamist leader and a few months later, another series of three television broadcasts "uncovered" terrible Islamist practices through discussions between repentant militants and religious scholars from al-Azhar on the lawn

9. Eberhard Kienle describes the crackdowns in the 1990s on Islamists from within the religious establishment that paralleled the media campaign: first the 1996 law restricting independent mosques by requiring preachers to be authorized by the Ministry of Religious Affairs and then the 1998 dissolution by the rector of al-Azhar (after investigation by the Ministry of Social Affairs) of the board of an increasingly conservative and Islamist association of scholars called the Front of the Scholars of al-Azhar *(jabhat 'ulama al-Azhar)*. Kienle, *A Grand Delusion: Democracy and Economic Reform in Egypt* (London: I.B. Tauris, 2001), 104-5, 113-14.

of a maximum security prison. Viewers were told that the repentant militants "wished to share their experiences with others to save them from falling into the 'spider's web' of terrorist groups." The prisoners talked about how the Islamist groups deliberately misinterpreted Islam to serve their lust for power (since violence, they reiterated, runs counter to Islam), misused funds, engaged in shady practices to satisfy sexual urges, and were obsessed with superficial matters such as veiling and makeup for women and beards for men.

When accused of failing to engage in true dialogue with Islamists in such staged events, the Minister of Information responded with a statement that takes us to the heart of the official construction of religion. He said, "[T]here are repenters who speak with remorse and provide an essential critique of their errors in understanding Islamic doctrine and participating in terrorist crimes. They discuss how it was that they came to understand the truth and lost their faith in those erroneous ideas that had led them to commit deviant terrorist activities. As such, they demonstrate, through their experiences, what constitutes false and sound thought." Making the distinction is key: serials like *The Family* contrast the good, correct, and reasonable Islam of the people, the cultured and educated, al-Azhar, the state, and television with the bad, violent, misinformed, twisted Islam of the extremists. The big Adel Imam film *The Terrorist*, released on the feast immediately following the Ramadan screening of *The Family*, sent a similar message. As Walter Armbrust, an anthropologist who also works on mass media in Egypt notes, it drew a stark distinction between modern enlightenment and Islamist backwardness, making the brainwashed fundamentalist character ignorant and barely literate, reading religious pamphlets about hellfire out loud, rocking back and forth "in an old-fashioned Quran-school style."[10] The policy paper of this media campaign asserts that combating terrorism and defending true religion are not contradictory. As the Minister of Information put it, "We are deepening authentic religion and promoting higher values to form a valid society capable of taking responsibility."

Some TV writers have criticized what they see as television's attempts to appease al-Azhar, and by extension, Islamists. Usama Anwar 'Ukasha has generally been the most outspoken in his criticism of state television's attempt to appease Islamists. Responding to the general increase in religious programs over the past couple of decades and the growing deference of the Egyptian Radio and Television Union to al-Azhar, he had written, "The policy of media confronta-

10. Walter Armbrust, "Islamists in Egyptian Cinema", *American Anthropologist* 104, no. 3 (2002): 922-31.

tion of extremism will not succeed simply by encouraging works that deal with extremism. It will succeed only if it ceases to attempt to demonstrate its religiosity... which has led... television to abdicate some of its basic rights, like the right to choose programs." Discussing a program that was submitted to al-Azhar and then censored, he asked, "Why are you placing a religious institution in a position of power and judgment in a matter that does not concern it?"

In the same year, the well-known director Muhammad Fadil actually blamed television's compromises for the spread of extremism. He said in an interview with me, "Egyptians have always been a religious people, without any outside interference, and without the excessive religiosity that is now present in the mass media. It is as if those responsible feel guilty, and thus the mass media feel the need to assert their religiosity. Why? ...We should resist this [apologetic] impulse and... limit the amount of religious programming on television." When I asked whether he thought extremism should be confronted through the media, as the Minister of Information had urged, he responded harshly, and with support for government policy that was uncharacteristic of this social critic who was known for targeting the government's neo-liberal economic policies in his serials. It was too late, he argued. "Today as a citizen, I don't feel safe walking in the street. I'm even afraid to go to the theatre or cinema. The situation has degenerated so much that it can no longer be confronted by art... [I]t is beyond being dealt with by words; it has to be dealt with forcefully with repressive security...."

These television writers are part of a minority who claim to be secularists – that is, they believe in a separation between personal piety and the state, a legacy of their intellectual and political formation in the Nasser period of the 1950s and 1960s, which pushed secular ideals. Yet, despite the objections of such prominent television personnel and their own relative silence on religion in their serials, Egyptian television continued to increase religious programming during the 1990s, adding to the popular shows featuring Quranic exegeses by religious authorities big budget serials about the history of the Arab-Islamic world. These were broadcast alongside many other serials with plots or subplots about violent militants and serials explicitly about terrorism. A good example of this is the serial broadcast in 1997 called *Dream of a Southerner.*

The moral authority of the religious establishment and pressure from below, including from professionals like doctors and lawyers sympathetic to the Islamist project in its more peaceful forms, have made it impossible for television, or the state, to stand against religion, or for secularism. The broad piety movement and the widespread feeling against cordoning off religion as a private matter of faith have led television to capitulate to the desire for more religious programming and to try to appropriate for itself the role of supporter of a legitimate Islam.

Egyptian state television respects the call to prayer and the religious calendar, offers Quranic exegesis and somber religious songs on the proper holidays even while entertaining viewers with the wild and attractive dancers of the traditional Ramadan riddle shows (*fawazir*), sexual innuendo in the classic black-and-white films of an earlier era, a growing industry of music videos, and, even flashy consumption in the increasingly slick advertisements for products promising the good life. These contradictions open television up to criticism from various quarters, since those who believe it would be a good thing to live in a society with Islamic mores are suspicious of certain forms of entertainment while many viewers (some the same) and sponsors seem to want the rest of what is transmitted.

The more serious problem for Egyptian television, when it is mobilized to fight terrorism or religious extremism, is that it risks offending large portions of the national community who may be against terrorism but are happy enough with other aspects of religiosity and Islamism. Not everyone accepts the television story that Islamists are "the other" within the nation. Many people are pious, not just poor, working women like the ones I knew who attend mosque lessons, but also middle-class professionals and even movie stars. Certainly almost everyone now has associates, friends, or relatives who have become insistently Islamic in their identities. Private Islamic schools preparing elite students have sprung up in Cairo and Alexandria, as anthropologist Linda Herrera[11] has shown. Teachers in state schools in Upper Egypt train their students not to use greetings common in the local dialect and to use instead the proper Islamic salutations. Many see greater adherence to Islamic law and morality as leading to the reform and restoration of the good society and nation, not its downfall.

Serials like *The Family*, which attempt to discredit Islamists, ironically provided the occasion for the expression of differences between those who see religious zeal as "extremism" and those who do not. Thus, rather than healing wounds in the national body, such didactic serials may actually work to expose them, with the heated debate in the press I have described indicating that such serials may lead to the public articulation of differences about the place of religion in society and the nation. However, it can still be argued that the serials and the debates about them do work to create national community in a more subliminal way, even when viewers resist the specific messages about extremists. The serials and the debates they provoke contribute to a shared construction in Egypt of religion

11. Herrera, Linda. (2001) Accomodating Disco and Quran: Lay Female Pedagogues and the Education of Metropolitan Muslims. In: *Muslim Traditions and Modern Techniques of Power*, Armando Salvatore (ed.), *Yearbook of the Sociology of Islam* (vol. 3), Hamburg: Lit Verlag, and New York: Transaction Books: 225-39.

as a sphere of beliefs and practices that can be wrong or right and whose believers can act excessively or moderately, in the right or wrong social spheres. There is good Islam and bad Islam and these judgments are made, ultimately, on the basis of how Islam relates to the nation and social responsibility. They are not, as they might have been in the past, part of the struggle among religious authorities. This is reflected in the Minister of Information's statement about the new policy of using media to confront terrorism, in which he talked about the need to teach authentic Islam and then, in the same document, called upon intellectuals to participate by "disseminating enlightenment and modernity, treating social problems in a balanced way, and encouraging people to remember the nation." The media campaigns, and mass media in general, reinforce a construction of religion as something distinct that pertains to the nation. This, we should admit, is a somewhat peculiar and historically specific vision of religion that gives body to the nation as the basic ground of experience and the measure of truth.

In relation to the larger question I raised at the beginning, however, what I want to point out is that the media discourse in Egypt that condemns terrorism or religious extremism objectifies and caricatures Islamists as much as the Western press does. But it is careful to set up an opposition not of a superior west that shares nothing with Islamists but a nation that embraces a moderate rational enlightened and truer form of Islam, one that is in the national interest. This is an internal struggle for the hearts and minds of Muslim citizens, not a production of alien Muslim monsters.

Muslims and Copts

In my book *Dramas of Nationhood*, I talk about a second strategy that television serials in the late 1990s followed to manage religious extremism. Noting the tensions between Muslims and Copts, and the growing extremism on both sides, several television serials from the late 1990s on, took up the theme of Muslim-Coptic amity and the need for unity, even if separate and different. This short text does not allow for a detailed description of this strategy and the television serials through which it was promoted, or the contentious public responses to these serials, but I will just say that what resulted was an ironic fixing of the communities as indeed quite distinct and separate and an exposure of divisions rather than an amelioration of them. Yet, I think I could show that these serials about religions and communalism contribute to something else that links them to the serials about Islamists: by drawing attention to the religious identities of characters and representing the religions in terms of the obvious formalities of dress or action, they contribute to the objectification of religion itself as a kind of cultural element. This rewrites religious distinctions as cultural differences, which leads the way for multicultural conceptions of religions as national subcultures, not opposing truths or political antagonists. The nation is presented as the framework within which religio-cultural difference occurs. Again, let us briefly point out the difference between this kind of representation of Christians and Muslims and those implied by the representation of the Muslim as outside the West (subliminally understood as Christian despite professed claims of either universalism or multiculturalism). Or the difference between this national framework and that which represents those Muslims present in the West, whether immigrants, citizens, visitors, or converts, as dangerous intruders.

Restoring the Honor of Upper Egypt

Let me now turn with a little more detail to the third strategy of Egyptian television serials that began in the late 1990s in dealing with Islamism. The classic association in the powerful urban centers of the north of religious strife with Upper Egypt (southern Egypt), like the condensation of the Islamist threat into that same disadvantaged region, was deliberately confronted in a number of late-1990s serials. For half a century, revenge, or the vendetta, has in the national imagination been the cultural trait most associated with Upper Egypt. The obsession by northern, urban, educated people with the horrors of the feud and their condemnation of Upper Egyptians as backward and unenlightened can be found everywhere, from film to social science. Without denying the existence or importance of this practice to communities in the region, one must still be suspicious whenever a cultural trait is singled out and made to stand for a whole region or community.

What is new since the 1990s when the Islamists began their campaign of targeting tourists, is that the clashes between security forces and Islamic groups, especially in Upper Egypt, where some of the major Pharaonic sites lie, have been labeled as vendetta, a cultural practice represented as destructive to human life and community, and even economic and social progress. When Islamic groups are understood as taking revenge on government forces for their having arrested or killed relatives, rather than engaging in an insurrection that is being repressed or constituting a social movement intent on changing the fundamental structures of governance and society to bring them in line with a vision of an Islamic society, their socio-political motivation is forced into a backward tradition with which no one should sympathize. The further implication is that Islamists are destroying the life and body of the nation, as is regularly said of feuding.

But it seems to me that something began to shift in the second half of the 1990s. The most popular of the serials to represent Upper Egypt balanced the theme of revenge with that of authentic values such as honor and integrity. The recent spate of serials set in Upper Egypt that depict positive qualities in that region are mostly the work of one writer, himself originally from Upper Egypt. Although based in Alexandria, Muhammad Safa' 'Amir makes much of the fact that he was born in an Upper Egyptian town not far from Luxor. Even those in the south point out that his work does not stereotype them negatively, further describing his serials as realistic because they focus on their "true" characteristics: generosity, courage, honesty, and valor.[12]

Although the sudden popularity of a television writer and his capitalization on a successful product through spin-offs surely explains part of this phenomenon of positive serials about Upper Egyptians, the timing in the wider context of the state's enlistment of media in its struggle against Islamists places the serials in a particular light. We might see them as trying to work rhetorically on audiences in two ways. For northerners, such as the millions of viewers in Cairo who loved them, these serials function as propaganda, enhancing the image of Upper Egyptians by disaggregating the population. Some groups and families are shown to have admirable qualities like valor, loyalty, and honor. They are struggling, as in one serial called *Diffuse Light*, which includes upstarts who resort to violence driven by material greed or the hunger for power or with Islamists masking the same motivations with religious zeal. Moreover, some of the serials reassuringly show that Upper Egyptians have links to the north; they travel back and forth and mix with northerners. This is historically true. What these serials suggest is that Sa'idis are part of the nation; they do not live in a closed society and do not constitute a backward or frightening "other." The most important message is that they are by no means all religious extremists.

Upper Egyptians, on the other hand, are being told that they have within their own traditions important values worth preserving and nurturing, values that are social, cultural, and regional, not particularly tied to religion. In other words, their true identities are not as Islamists but rather as people with an indigenous regional nobility and code of honour. From my fieldwork in Upper Egypt I would

12. Mahmud Musa, "Al-sura al-namatiyya li-l-sa'idi" (The modal image of the Upper Egyptian), *Al-Ahram* February 18, 1996.

say that this message was widely appreciated by locals. Although many people told me how hilarious they found the dialects and expressions, they were quite forgiving. Their appreciation of the positive image of Upper Egyptians was clear in the response to *Fugitive from Love*, the serial broadcast during Ramadan in 2000-2001. People I knew in the region were thrilled that it was filmed in recognizable locales on the east and west banks of the Nile around Luxor, where they lived. The key to its popularity was revealed, however, in one young woman's description. "This serial really enhanced the reputation of Upper Egyptians," she said. She claimed that the message the serial was conveying was that Sa'idis are tough and honorable, "real men," as she said. She described how government officials in the serial were shocked that the Sa'idis stood up to them. When the government minister's son wanted them to sell him some land that they did not have the rights to, the Sa'idi mayor challenged him by saying, "You can remove me [from office] if you want but I won't go along with your scheme." Another young woman I spoke with about the serial, described another episode with a similar message. She was impressed with how the mayor's son responded when the young professional woman (with ancestry in the region) who had been brought up in Alexandria accused him of stealing the deed to her land. He had said, "I wouldn't do something like that. I'm a Sa'idi!"

Although attempting to restore the honor of Upper Egypt, linking Upper Egyptians to the rest of the Egyptians, and offering rural Upper Egyptian traditional values as an alternative to Islamism, these prominent serials nevertheless relied on the difference between north and south for their meaning. They sustained stereotypes of clannishness, of patriarchal custom, and of codes of revenge in Upper Egypt. And by associating a certain enlightenment with educated northerners and those from the south who have redeemed themselves through education (as in *Dream of the Southerner* about a self-taught local Egyptologist), they reaffirmed, in the conventional language of social progress, the inferiority of the underprivileged region. The serials thus confirmed, even in their more positive depiction of the south, the distance Upper Egyptians experience regularly between themselves and those from the north, especially during direct encounters.

The serials did not weaken local regional identity, an identity especially apparent among those who have not been through the nationalistic school system. An incident that depends on the ambiguity of "*Misr*" the word for both the nation, Egypt, and Cairo (and by extension the heavily populated north of Egypt) illustrates this continuing local identification. When I was telling one family the story of how we had asked permission from our children's school principal in the US to take them to Egypt (I used the word "*Misr*"), the smart but uneducated mother laughed sharply. "Are we *Misr*? This isn't *Misr*!" She seemed genuinely surprised when her educated son then patiently explained, "Yes, mother. This is *Misr* too – from Aswan to Alexandria."

Even if the serials about Upper Egypt did not, in fact, undermine regional differences, they were meant to have performed the important function of affirming Sa'idi values, not the newer ones that have swept the region, inspiring mosque building and intolerance. Here again, there is certainly some fit between the serials and the experiences of locals, especially in the part of Upper Egypt that depends heavily on tourism for its economic survival. The community in which I worked was shaken badly by the 1997 massacre of tourists at the Pharaonic temple of Queen Hatchepsut, in the nearby valley.

The rage and horror people felt was expressed perfectly by one young woman's insistence that these terrorists were "not Muslims, not Christians, not of any religion. They were not even human if they could do such a thing." Despite this heartfelt condemnation of the incident and the Islamists who perpetrated it, people in this region are nevertheless sympathetic to many forms of strong Islamic identity, from popular to reformist. Some examples give a sense of the variety of forms this takes. There has long been a major religious figure in the area with a wide following and enormous local respect as a mediator and leader.[13] Similarly, the *moulids* (saint's day celebrations) of major and minor figures are well attended, the Sufi brotherhoods organizing *dhikrs* as well. Observers have also noted that more orthodox religious observance (Ramadan fasting, mosque attendance, and criticism of alcohol) has been steadily increasing over the last twenty years. Religious education is considered useful, a good portion of the local children going, for varied reasons, to the parallel school system run by al-Azhar. Many children are sent to a Quranic teacher (*kuttab*) in the afternoons and summer holidays. There was, among all the people I knew, a keen consciousness of religious identity and a commitment to the morality of that identity.

It is not just in terms of its reinforcement of the differences between north and south but also in its elision of a positive Islamic identity for the region, that television drama's third strategy of recuperating some sort of Upper Egyptian culture as a way to unite the nation, forge community, and fight terrorism is, it would seem, not without problems and resistances. The audiences for such televi-

13. See Rachida Chih, *Le Soufisme au Quotidien: Confréries d'Egypte au XXe Siècle* (Arles: Actes Sud - Sindbad, 2000); and Valerie Hoffman, *Sufism, Mystics, and Saints in Modern Egypt* (Columbia, SC: University of South Carolina Press, 1995)

sion programs, even if encouraged to be proud of their Upper Egyptian heritage, would be loath to see themselves as only Upper Egyptians, and not also good Muslims – or Copts, for that matter.

Media's attempts to promote a culture stripped of religion may have even less of a healing effect on the torn body than its attempts to turn religion into a cultural system linked to the nation, as in the second strategy. This is because it bears little resemblance to local experiences. But insofar as regional values are offered as cultural ideals in the serials, a national framework is invoked, since regions are defined by national territory. Upper Egypt only has meaning as a distinct region if it is understood as being part of a larger Egyptian nation. And so again, we find support for a united nation and a placing of religion within that nation.

Religion in a National Public Sphere

So, what can we conclude from our close look at television soap operas in Egypt? I have tried to show that the diverse contents of and contentious responses to the serials mobilized against terrorism and religious extremism since the mid-1990s should not distract us from the commonalities that underlie them and the commonplaces they reinforce. In this paper, I have presented the serials as vehicles for carrying messages and the press as a sphere in which political debate about such messages occurs. Recent work on Islamism and the history of Muslim reform in Egypt reminds us that we should treat mass media, from the press that flourished in the late-nineteenth century to the television of the late-twentieth century, as part of a distinct public sphere in which public intellectuals could debate and discuss norms, policies, and the future of the community and civilization. Scholars have been concerned about what the outlines of this public sphere are and how the changing terms of debate and discussion were set.

The intelligentsia, who produce television, film, theatre, and literature in Egypt must be understood as having a certain independence from the state and laboring to a large extent in their own cultural fields. Yet there are significant points of collaboration and convergence between intellectuals and the state. The debates in the public sphere about religious extremism make clear that the basis of this collaboration is the national interest. This would seem to represent a significant departure from the initial formation of the public sphere in the nineteenth century, as described by Armando Salvatore, Skovgaard-Petersen, and other scholars. Salvatore argues that nationalist discourse eclipsed Islamic reform as the ideological hub of the public sphere in the 1920s.[14] Nasserism would contribute even more definitively to the doctrine of a demarcation of separate spheres of religion and state, even if Islamic ideals were never purged from morality, pious practices continued among all the classes, and various accommodations were made between state and religious institutions. What we seem to be seeing now in the debates in which television programs of the 1990s participated, is that religion has again become an ideological hub of the public sphere, but with a certain form of the modern nation-state so entrenched and established that "the nation," and what is good for the nation, now form the only legitimate grounds for debates about religion. This is so even when viewers explicitly disagree with or criticize the representations of Islamists, or religiosity, that they watch.

The airing of these serials ends up, in a variety of ways, revealing and exacerbating social cleavages, perhaps undermining the government's and some secular intellectuals' intentions of creating national community by trying to discredit Islamists. This is because television's enthusiasm for circumscribing religious sensibilities in its serials rubs up against widespread convictions. However, one should not infer from these failures that television does not foster national community through its treatments of religious extremism. It does so indirectly, though, by appropriating for itself the role of a charged and popular arena for public discussion of and debate about Islam. The arena is national and in this way contributes to an ongoing sense of the nation as the critical frame for all aspects of life, including the religious. Here we might think that we should reverse the title of a book by Dale Eickelman and Jon Anderson on media. They called their book *New Media in the Muslim World* (Bloomington: Indiana University Press, 1999). I think we should talk about "new Islam in a media world."

But finally, to return to the main theme of this paper, we must keep in mind that Egyptian television's negative stereotyping of Islamists, however accepted or rejected by the public, operates within, and reinforces, the framework of the nation. In doing that, it never places the Muslim outside the frame. Instead it makes distinctions between good and bad Muslims. It reflects on what place religious identity and observance should have in daily life. It asks what role Islam should have in society at large. It even asks whether Islamists are fit to govern. So, even though some of the imagery used to represent Islamists may be eerily similar to that which is becoming numbingly familiar in the West, the contexts of reception and the import of this imagery give it a fundamentally different meaning.

14. Armando Salvatore, "Introduction: The Problem of the Ingraining of Civilizing Traditions into Social Governance," in *Muslim Traditions and Modern Techniques of Power*, Yearbook of the Sociology of Islam 3, ed. Salvatore (Munster: LIT Verlag, 2001), 9-42, quote from 19.

Lila Abu-Lughod is Professor of Anthropology and Director of the Institute for Research on Women and Gender at Columbia University, New York. As an anthropologist, she has been concerned about the politics of representation, developing a critique of the concept of culture. She has also written widely on gender and popular culture in the Middle East. Among her publications are: *Veiled Sentiments: Honor and Poetry in a Bedouin Society* (Berkeley: University of California Press, 1986/2000); *Writing Women's Worlds: Bedouin Stories* (Berkeley: University of California Press, 1993); *Remaking Women: Feminism and Modernity in the Middle East,* edited (Princeton: Princeton University Press, 1998); *Media Worlds: Anthropology on New Terrain,* co-edited (Berkeley: University of California Press, 2002); and *Dramas of Nationhood: The Politics of Television in Egypt* (University of Chicago Press, 2005).

INTERNATIONAL INSTITUTE
FOR THE STUDY OF ISLAM
IN THE MODERN WORLD (ISIM)

Visiting address:
Rapenburg 59
2311 GJ Leiden
The Netherlands

Postal address:
P.O. Box 11089
2301 EB Leiden
The Netherlands

Telephone:
+31-(0)71-527 79 05

Fax:
+31-(0)71-527 79 06

E-mail:
info@isim.nl

Website:
www.isim.nl